BE ENCOURAGED

MENTORING AND THE PROPHETIC

BY JOHN O'SHAUGHNESSY

PUBLISHED BY

ELGIN, ILLINOIS

**BE ENCOURAGED:
MENTORING AND THE PROPHETIC**

by John O'Shaughnessy

Copyright©2008 by Praiseworthy Ministry
All Rights Reserved

This publication or parts of it may not be reproduced in any form, stored in any retrieval system or transmitted in any form without prior written permission of Praiseworthy Ministry, except as allowed by United States of America copyright law.

Published by This Joy! Books
P.O. Box 823, Elgin, IL 60121
A Division of Three Cord Ministries
Milwaukee Avenue, Libertyville, IL
www.thisjoy.com

Thank you to Sam Storms for permission to share about your influence.
Thank you to Jimmy Stewart, author of the article "The Man Behind Michael," *Charisma*, April 2000, pg. 54-55. Used by permission.

Written with the help of Ginny Emery, This Joy! Books, Elgin, Illinois.
Cover design by Gretchen Stibolt, The Design Desk, Nashville, Tennessee.

Unless otherwise indicated, Scripture is taken from the HOLY BIBLE, NEW INTERNATIONAL VERSION®. Copyright © 1973, 1978, 1984 International Bible Society. Used by permission of Zondervan. All rights reserved.

The "NIV" and "New International Version" trademarks are registered in the United States Patent and Trademark Office by International Bible Society. Use of either trademark requires the permission of International Bible Society.

Scripture verses marked NKJV are taken from the New King James Version. Copyright © 1982 by Thomas Nelson, Inc. Used by permission. All rights reserved.

International Standard Book Number: 978-0-9821835-0-2

Printed in the United States of America

Dedication

*It is with a grateful heart that I wish to dedicate
this booklet to two of my mentors
in hearing God's voice.
They were brought into my life
as true gifts from God.*

*Jim Gochenour taught me so much.
I am forever indebted to his patience and humility.*

*I also want to acknowledge my friend Jim Goll.
What wonderful memories I carry
from the days he took me on ministry trips.
But his friendship impacted me more
than the trips and the training!
Thank you, Jim.*

ENDORSEMENTS

John's experience and stories will inspire you to mentor and be mentored. He passes on what he has learned in the way the Apostle Paul instructed Timothy to do in 2 Timothy 2:1-2, "You therefore, my son, be strong in the grace that is in Christ Jesus and the things that you have heard from me among many witnesses, commit these to faithful men who will be able to teach others also." *Be Encouraged* will motivate the body of Christ to mature in the gift of prophecy.

Linda and Ed Hackett
International House of Prayer, Kansas City, Missouri

My wife Anne and I have known John and Caryl for over a decade. They have helped us grow in the prophetic and in intimacy with God in ways we never imagined possible. This booklet is a great tool to help you along your prophetic journey.

Michael Risher
Sr. V. P. Investments, Advisory & Brokerage Services

John and Caryl O'Shaughnessy brought a dimension to our relationship with Jesus that would not have existed without them. The richness of our walk and our understanding of how the Lord speaks to His children is because of what they sowed into our lives. We are grateful beyond words for all the Lord brought to us through their ministry.

Dawn and Dave Mitchell
Friends of Praiseworthy Ministry

John O'Shaughnessy presents a compelling case for the need for mentors to call forth and nurture the prophetic spirit in the lives of believers. Through hands-on involvement, John and Caryl have experienced firsthand the joy and delight of growing in their gifting under the watchful eye of spiritual mothers and fathers who have cared for the heart of the individual as much as for the gifting that is resident within. We recommend this booklet for anyone who is seeking a safe environment in which to begin their journey in the prophetic.

Carol and Wes Hall
International House of Prayer, Kansas City, Missouri

There are very few fathers/mentors in the prophetic world. John O'Shaughnessy is one of the best. He has been a mentor to me, both up close and from a distance. He has saved me from so many "fumbles." Learn from his stories, his real life experiences. He'll help you to miss many of the potholes we find ourselves in as we learn and grow. When I have questions, when I get lost in my prophetic gifting, John has been there for me—and now you too can *Be Encouraged!*

Marty O'Connor
Ministry Consultant, Holland, Michigan

BEGINNINGS

My Dad's heart was turned toward me. He'd get up to help me on my paper route at five in the morning. He coached my baseball team and drove me to hockey games for ten years. He was my first mentor. He loved me and provided for me.

My Dad died in 2000, but I still look for him once in a while when I see a stranger in a crowd tilt his head a certain way. I wonder if he smiles on the succession of mentors God has given me. I've certainly needed them.

I began to prophesy with almost no understanding of what I was doing or how to do it. I still wince when I think back to the first time I intentionally prophesied in a church setting. I spoke directly to the pastor. I wasn't sure what his reaction was going to be. It was our first Sunday at the church, so we didn't know each other. Even though the word was encouraging, it felt awkward, and some of what I shared made no sense to me.

Thankfully, the pastor took it in stride and gently smiled back at me. We all have to start somewhere. Little did I know that my toe was on the starting line of a long learning curve. Looking back, I recognize and openly admit many mistakes; they were not made out of rebellion or anger, but simply from immaturity. I would have stumbled more if God had not given me mentors for each new season in my development.

WHO NEEDS A MENTOR?

If you're just beginning to discover your spiritual gifts and calling, you may think that you don't need a mentor—that the only real mentor is the Holy Spirit. I understand that. He is the ultimate mentor.

In *The Beginner's Guide to Hearing God* (Scottsdale, AZ: Regal, 2004), my friend Jim Goll says this about the Holy Spirit:

> *The Holy Spirit is our counselor and our teacher, yet He is more than a teacher—more like a tutor. But He is not just any tutor; He's the kind who truly loves to spend individual, personal time with each of His students. He is like that rare kind of guidance counselor who actually becomes a friend. He is like the teacher who becomes a personal mentor.* (p.24)

The balanced truth, however, is that the Holy Spirit often chooses to work through people. What are pastors and teachers if they are not mentors, makers of disciples who pass on what they have learned to others so the church may grow in unity and maturity?

Through watching the wonderful mentors God has given to me and through the grace He's given me to mentor others, I've discovered that seeking a mentor and looking for opportunities to mentor others is a key way to develop your own giftings and to draw closer to Jesus and your destiny in Him.

As God continues to pour out His Spirit on all people and to unfold His gifts, these gifts need to be nurtured.

> *And afterward, I will pour out my Spirit on all people. Your sons and daughters will prophesy, your old men*

will dream dreams, your young men will see visions. Even on my servants, both men and women, I will pour out my Spirit in those days. (Joel 2: 28-29)

It's pretty clear from these verses that God is pouring out His Spirit and that He will continue to do so in the coming days. In the last decade, I've met many people who are dreaming dreams, seeing visions and beginning to prophesy. When I first met some of these people, they did not even believe that these gifts were available today. Over the years, I have watched many of them grow up into amazing spiritual maturity. Those who sought mentors usually stayed the course. We need to have mentors in place, especially prophetic mentors, to help those new in the gift of prophecy grow and mature.

Looking over the church landscape for expressions of the Kingdom of God, I see a need for the seeds that God has planted within people to germinate and take root, to be watered and cared for—and I see mentoring as a way to accomplish this.

My own passion revolves around prophetic mentoring, most importantly mentoring the next generation to hear God's voice and to speak out what they hear.

Why is mentoring so important, especially prophetic mentoring? It may have something to do with our need for a Father's love, a parent's acceptance. Paul wrote:

Even though you have ten thousand guardians in Christ, you do not have many fathers, for in Christ Jesus I became your father through the gospel. (1 Corinthians 4:15)

As much as Caryl and I are able, the Lord has put it in our hearts to "father and mother" the young adults God brings into our lives. Recently, the Lord spoke to me and said, "Prophetic mentoring is one of the best ideas I ever gave you, John." It hit me like a ton of bricks to realize that mentoring wasn't "my" idea but His, one He deposited in me.

Those still young in prophetic ministry need encouragement and "gentle nudges" in the right directions. It makes my wife, Caryl, and me happy to share our stories with people. Perhaps learning from our experiences and examples will bring them further along than they might travel alone.

We feel that way because of our own experience. Whenever we reached a crossroad on our Christian journey, God sent the right person to encourage us, walk with us, and pray with us. These mentors helped us grow exponentially in our prophetic giftings. I don't believe that the best way to learn about prophetic ministry has to by trial and error. There is a better way!

Just recently, Caryl and I started a prophetic mentoring group at the International House of Prayer in Kansas City. The group meets in our home; we talk together, encourage those who come, and become cheerleaders for people wanting to hear God's voice. We want to help and bless God's sons and daughters in prophecy. As time permits, we want to start more groups.

THE MOTIVATION OF REJECTED PROPHETS

Our experience has not been the norm. Unfortunately, Mike Bickle's description of the motivation of rejected prophets in *Growing in the Prophetic* (Lake Mary, FL: Charisma House, 1996) is far more common. He writes:

Be Encouraged

> *Most prophetic people get in touch with their giftings long before they cultivate the corresponding wisdom, humility and character that is necessary to succeed in prophetic ministry. In the beginning, they may appear arrogant or pushy because of their zeal. As years go by, their pushiness usually comes from fear, hurt and rejection. Most prophetic people who have been around for a few years have had their hands slapped many times. Some of them have been dealt with harshly, without proper explanation and without the security of a good relationship with church leadership. The average person who had been in the prophetic ministry for ten years is pretty beat up and bruised. This is especially true if the prophetic gift was active in his or her early years.*

I remember reading this paragraph in Mike's book for the first time, many years ago. I asked myself the question, "Does a prophetic person REALLY have to be subjected to all this hurt and misunderstanding?" This must change!

On my ministry trips people often tell me sad stories about how they've been mistreated and misunderstood because of their prophetic gifting. Many are tired and worn out—on the brink of calling it quits. We've met some who quit ministering in their revelatory gifts because of discouragement, and we've met some who have left the ministry completely. This is tragic. Occasionally I get a phone call from a prophetic person who is considering giving up.

I listen with empathy: I, too, have gone through periods of deep discouragement. The difference is that I had mothers and fathers in the faith to assist me through tough times. My heart goes out to help as I've been helped.

AVOIDING MISTAKES

By God's grace, Caryl and I have been spared many bumps and bruises. In listening to others tell their stories, I've learned how timely support and wise counsel have helped us, and I've seen how mentoring might have spared others from hurt and rejection. Because I know from experience how much proper coaching helped us to navigate through rough waters, mentoring is close to my heart.

Most of the mistakes I've seen prophetic people make are what I would call honest mistakes, unintentional errors made from confusion, inexperience or ignorance.

I recall one of my mistakes. I was driving down the highway and thought the Lord was asking me to get off at the next exit and go into a particular restaurant. I sensed that I would meet a thirty-five-year-old man and that God wanted me to pray for him. Trying to be obedient, I exited the highway, went into the restaurant and approached a man sitting off in a corner. He seemed younger than thirty-five to me, but I walked up, said hello and then asked him if he was thirty-five years old. He frowned, said no, and quickly left!

I was confused. I had been so sure I'd heard God correctly. Evidently, I had not! In my zeal and immaturity, I'd made a mistake. Mentors who believed in me shared stories of their own mistakes and helped to hold me steady. This embarrassing moment didn't make me want to quit trying to hear from God; it made me want to hear more clearly. We should never stop trying, even when we fail.

When I began learning to hear God's voice, I figured that if God was speaking to me about a person, or if I had a dream about someone, He wanted me to share it right away.

Over the years I have learned that revelation needs to be simmered in prayer. Then, when God releases the message, it's much more powerful and effective. Years ago I met a man and promised to pray for him. We did not see each other for ten years, but I kept on praying for him.

One day he called and said that he was going to be driving through Kansas City and wanted to see me. We met and had ten years of catching up to do! Near the end of our conversation, I told him that I had a word for him, and I'd been praying about it for the last ten years. I'll never forget the look in his eyes. He could not believe I'd continued praying. The word I'd saved and prayed about applied to an important business decision his company was in the process of making at that very time. The point is that a prophetic word is to be shared "when God instructs you to share it," not necessarily as soon as you get it. Frankly, that is the longest I've ever held on to a word before sharing it.

Timing is crucial. Sometimes God wants His revelations shared immediately. Sometimes I've prayed for more than a year before speaking. At first, waiting was difficult, but as I've drawn closer to God, it's become easier for Him to direct me. I'm confident that as you pray and seek God, He will let you know when to speak and when to be still.

PRINCIPLES

Just knowing and following a few simple principles can save us from embarrassing others and ourselves. One principle is: don't presume about timing but *ask God* for His timing. Don't trust your own intuitions. **Ask!** If you could listen in on my conversations with the Holy Spirit about timing, you might think they're silly, but again and again He's helped me.

One conversation went something like this: "Lord? You're telling me that Jack is getting into a sticky relationship and You want to help him out! Shall I confront him?"

"Oh. You want me to pray and then take him out to lunch next week for a heart to heart talk?"

After lunch with Jack, I was saying something like,

"Oh Boy, that's complex. I'm glad I didn't blurt out what you showed me. Thank you, Father."

Another principle is to hold steady and keep your mouth closed, tightly and forever, if you receive an insight that God tells you to pray about and never share. Surprisingly, God trusts prophetic gifts to ordinary people like you and me who have no training or experience. More than once I've have conversations that ran something like this:

You're going to do WHAT, Lord? I don't believe it. But it sounds like You. And you don't want me to tell anyone because they wouldn't believe it either? They'd mock the gift of prophecy? They wouldn't honor you? Oh. Why are you telling me?

A third principle is to accept that God's ways are mysterious. He doesn't always tell us what to do. Prophetic men and women sometimes have no idea what to do with their insights or why God has chosen to give them His revelation. His ways and His purposes are entirely His own.

Sometimes we need to actually see God's ways in the lives of others; it's not enough be told about them. Understanding comes through friendships with men and women who live close to His Spirit. In other words, His ways are caught, not taught. That's one reason I often pray that God will increase the number of moms and dads in prophetic ministry. They are needed to help train the young ones. That's also why I'm writing this booklet—to urge every young person reading it to seek a mentor!

HEART MOTIVATIONS AND REWARDS

If God ever asks me to live out the rest of my life mentoring people behind the scenes, I would consider it a joy and would do it in a second. Frankly, I find more joy in encouraging individuals or mentoring in small groups than I get on the platform giving prophetic words. Don't get me wrong, I love the conferences and seminars, but I am convinced that impacting a person's life in any significant way is best accomplished face to face. Because I've received the most and learned the most in small group settings, I always want to place myself where I can build relationships that will encourage others to listen for God's voice for themselves. It's often easier to hear from God through someone else. It's different when you have to listen for Him yourself.

When Caryl and I mentor, we get involved in people's lives. We begin to care about their growth and maturity and want them to fully develop their gifts. We go to God for them in prayer. It often feels as though we grow more than those we nurture, and we receive much more than we give. When we are mentoring someone, we sometimes feel a bit as Paul felt toward the Colossians.

> *We ... do not cease to pray for you, and to ask that you may be filled with the knowledge of His will in all wisdom and spiritual understanding; that you may walk worthy of the Lord, fully pleasing* Him, *being*

fruitful in every good work and increasing in the knowledge of God. (Colossians 1:9-10, NKJV)

WHAT IS MENTORING?

There are many definitions of mentoring. The one I like the best is taken from the book *Connecting* by Paul Stanley and Robert Clinton (Colorado Springs, CO: NavPress, 1992). They define mentoring as

> *... a relational experience through which one person empowers another by sharing God-given resources. The resources vary. Mentoring is a positive dynamic that enables people to develop potential.* (p. 12)

My own definition of mentoring is loving and encouraging someone while trying to help develop their God-given talents.

Mentoring starts when someone has a need and another person is willing to provide assistance. It's all about developing relationships and empowering others. God did not make us to be self-sufficient. Mentoring flows out of a desire to see others grow in knowledge and in understanding of who they are in Christ. I look at mentoring as being along a continuum. Some mentoring takes place in a very deliberate fashion, sometimes it is ongoing, and other times it is occasional.

DELIBERATE MENTORING

I was once so desperate for a mentor that I prayed and asked God to show me whom to ask. I felt God was showing me that Dr. Sam Storms would help me for a season. It took me weeks to get up the courage to ask him because I thought he'd be too busy. Now I can look back and laugh at my feelings. Here's what happened. Although I wanted a mentor, I did not want to bother Sam. I assumed that since he didn't know me well, he'd automatically say no to my request. The day came when I finally built up enough courage to drive to his office. I nervously walked into his reception area half expecting him to be in some important meeting, unable to see me.

His wife, Ann, was at the reception desk and greeted me with a smile. She told me to walk right into his office. I felt lightheaded as I opened the door, and my mind went blank, even though I'd rehearsed my request many times. Somehow I got the words out. Much to my surprise, he agreed immediately. We would meet once a month for an hour. In those meetings I asked him many questions and hung onto every word he said! He was very understanding and patient with me. I look back on those times with fond memories. He encouraged me; he believed in me; and his faith helped me to believe more in myself. When the season with him came to an end, his interest motivated me to find another mentor and to look for someone I could mentor as well.

ONGOING MENTORING

I would describe this as a type of parent-child relationship. If there's a person in your life whom you see frequently and whose opinion you value highly, he or she might be a great person to ask to mentor you. An ongoing mentor might even be your own father, mother or friend. The main criteria for an ongoing mentor is that they be accessible and someone with whom you feel comfortable.

OCCASIONAL MENTORING

An occasional mentor might be a person from another city or state whom you see a few times a year or occasionally talk with on the phone. At one time, I traveled to Illinois and Michigan quite regularly and on each visit met with some of the same people. We just hung out together: there was no formal mentoring agreement, but God used me as their sounding board. I was more than happy to make myself available. I didn't realize the impact this had on some of them until later.

Occasional mentoring also works on ministry trips. It is fun to include others in the ministry portion of the meetings. Reading books about prophetic ministry, hearing teachings, and being mentored are of value, but there comes a time for all of us when we just have to DO IT! I often include others on trips to give them opportunities for hands-on experience. Others included me as I began to minister prophetically, and it was a powerful way to learn.

WHAT IS A MENTOR?

Bobb Biehl says it this way:

> *Mentoring is sort of tough, but describing it is pretty easy. It's like having an uncle that cares for you for a lifetime and wants to see you do well. He's not your competitor, he's there to support you, not to compete with you or discourage you. He's not your critic as much as he is your cheerleader.* (*Mentoring,* Nashville: Broadman and Holman, 1996)

After hearing that definition of a mentor I had only one question, *Who wouldn't want one?* No matter what spiritual gifts God has placed within us, the presence of a mentor is powerful; the gift of a good mentor is priceless.

BIBLICAL METHODS

Mentoring is not a new concept. Jesus mentored his twelve disciples. Can you imagine walking with Jesus, watching Him perform miracles, seeing Him cast out demons and raise the dead? Talk about valuable ministry experience! Jesus carefully selected a handful of men and poured His life into them. He and His disciples worked together, ministered together, traveled together, laughed, argued, ate, and prayed together. Jesus taught them, imparting Himself to them. He loved them and warned them of impending dangers. In my opinion, this is mentoring at its finest. Mentoring is all about relationships: it's also about the transforming power of friendship.

There are many biblical models of mentoring. One of my favorites is Elijah and Elisha. It is close to my heart because it is a model of prophetic mentoring. It illustrates how God uses weak and broken people to achieve His purposes. Elijah, the prophet, was discouraged and depressed (1 Kings 19). God's solution for Elijah was not a two-week vacation on the beach. His instructions were to go find a "son." God did not want Elijah's spiritual legacy to die. Elijah obeyed and trained Elisha to be his successor.

We read in 1 Kings 19:19 that Elijah placed his coat on Elisha and anointed him as his assistant. As Elisha was being mentored by Elijah, he grew in his prophetic gifting. At one point Elisha asks Elijah for a double portion of the spirit that was on him. True mentors must live with the expectation that their "sons and daughters" will go much further in God than they ever have gone. Elijah understood and gladly gave to Elisha.

In the Bible we see mentoring as a way of life. It was the primary way of handing down skills and wisdom from one generation to the next. Why shouldn't it be the same today? Unfortunately, there is a shortage of mentors throughout the body of Christ; far too many believers do not have access to a mentor. This is especially true within prophetic circles. Because very few prophetic people have made themselves available to mentor others, few have found mentors.

BEING MENTORED, OUR EXPERIENCES

An older couple, Jim and Joyce Gochenour, mentored Caryl and me. Jim was a retired fireman, and Joyce was a stay-at-home mom and grandma. Both Jim and Joyce were prophetically gifted, and we were blessed to be their friends. Caryl and I loved being with them. They frequently heard from God and were among our biggest cheerleaders.

What I appreciated most about Jim and Joyce was their ability to listen. Sometimes I would go to their house during the week and talk for hours about the ways God was directing Caryl and me. Inevitably, Joyce would serve cookies and milk or invite me to stay for lunch. She had such a gentle way about her. Everyone loved her. She and Jim heaped love on us and gave us a deeper understanding of prophetic ministry. It would not be an overstatement to say that Caryl and I hung onto every word they spoke. They had a wisdom beyond any we had ever seen.

On Fridays they hosted a prophetic nurturing group in their home. This group was the incubator that hatched our prophetic ministry! It was a safe place to practice hearing God's voice and to begin ministering to other people. Some nights thirty people crowded into their living room. Every person in the group was a beginner and very eager to learn how to hear God's voice. Meetings would typically begin with Jim sharing a few stories to build our faith. Eyes turned to God, and then worship would start. Finally, we would divide into small groups and pray for each other.

In our early years of learning about prophetic ministry, we took two trips with the Gochenours. These trips gave us many opportunities to practice our gifts and to hone our skills. The hands-on training we received was invaluable.

More important than any training we received, they loved us. They had a way of making us feel loved and important. The Bible tells us that without love spiritual gifts are worthless. The Gochenours' love was woven into every ministry opportunity they gave us. That's why, at the risk of repeating myself, I must emphasize it.

I felt I could do no wrong in Jim's sight as he smiled and nodded his approval. The love and affirmation we received kept our emotional and spiritual tanks FULL. Many times when we questioned our next move, Jim would share a word that not only gave us direction, but also greatly encouraged us. Just spending time with Jim and Joyce boosted our confidence. They literally lavished love on us. They impacted us in such a powerful way that mentoring became a priority for me. I knew that someday I would give what I had received and help others grow in their prophetic giftings.

ANOTHER EXAMPLE

At another season in our lives, Jim and Michal Ann Goll became precious mentors. We saw them following Jesus and learned from them. The time we spent just asking Jim and Michal Ann questions opened our eyes to far more than we could have ever learned on our own. We learned almost as much by observing them minister as we did by doing it ourselves. How they shared with us and helped us with practical information and advice has marked us in ways we can't even describe or fully comprehend. We know the power that comes from mentoring—we have tasted it!

We once traveled with the Golls to Austria where Jim was teaching at a conference in a small town called Wiener Neustadt, about an hour south of Vienna. This was exciting for us, and we were thankful to be part of the team. For me, the most profound part of the trip was Caryl's first speaking engagement. On previous trips, when I'd spoken, she'd prayed for me. Now it was her chance to speak and my opportunity to pray. How exciting that it happened to be at an international conference! We taught together in a workshop called, "How to Receive Revelation." It was well received, and working with an interpreter was definitely a new experience for both of us. I felt like that trip was worth five years of experience.

WHO QUALIFIES?

Mentoring has nothing to do with age or experience. It has to do with being realistic about who God is and who we are. Some of my hair is turning gray, but I still want mentors to teach me about the intricacies of prophetic ministry and hearing God's voice. I will always be a student of prophecy. There is always more to learn about hearing God's voice; there is always more knowledge to gain, new insights to see, new treasures to discover. I've learned that God does not always use the one who looks the most mature; God is looking to use the person who is most teachable, the one who who is most available and obedient.

I know my limitations. Others have more biblical knowledge and more degrees and are better teachers. But not all of these people have a prophetic gifting or ministry. During the early years, I would frequently ask God to find someone better suited, someone more educated to do this "prophetic ministry stuff." I felt so weak and without confidence that I begged God to find someone else! God did not give up on me. Neither did our mentors. When I became a Christian, I did not sign up for prophetic ministry. It's a calling I know I am not worthy of, but He gave it to me in spite of myself. Looking back, it's been by God's grace that we have persevered for almost twenty years.

HOLD ONTO GOD'S CALLINGS

Pray and ask God for a mentor. It may take time to recognize the right person, but don't give up. Continue to ask God to mature you and refine you. The Lord has a very special way of helping us by setting people in place who can see the truth for us when we can't. It's not always easy to believe in ourselves. Usually we need someone who can believe in us first. Our mentors did this for us. Mentors build into us so we can flow in the truth of our destiny. Mentors build up the body of Christ. Mentors are disciples, fishers of men. In Matthew 4:19 Jesus says, "Follow me, and I will make you fishers of men." Disciples follow Jesus, and we follow them as they follow Him.

Romans 11:29 says, "For the gifts and calling of God are irrevocable." This is an amazing promise from the Father. With this promise there are some major things to remember. First, God never takes back what He gives us; He keeps His promises. He will give us enabling grace to fulfill every promise He makes. Isn't that wonderful? Second, God's callings are much higher than we can see. We have no idea what eternal means. It's so huge our minds can't contain the knowledge of it now. Because of this we must remember not to quit, but to press into what God has imparted into our spirits for the benefit of building His Church.

God's gifts and callings aren't the same as being mature in character; they don't indicate how close we are to Him. As we seek God, we must trust Him to mature our gifts and character. We can't measure where we are by our own understanding. Wherever we may think we are today, it's no measure of how close we can come to our Heavenly Father.

None of us will ever reach completion until He comes back and fulfills the great promise. Revelation 22:17 says,

> *And the Spirit and the bride say, "Come!" And let him who hears say, "Come!" And let him who thirsts come. Whoever desires, let him take the water of life freely.* (NKJV)

The Holy Spirit is building the church to be Jesus' eternal bride. So do not grow weary in your particular spot today. Know that this same Holy Spirit who filled Jesus is with you completely. He stands for you and for the fulfillment of His eternal promises. He has promises for you, promises that no one else down here on earth, and no one who has ever lived on earth before you, and no one who will ever be born after you can fulfill. God will fulfill His promises to you in ways unique to you and for you alone. You were created for an eternal purpose with an eternal calling that will only be satisfied as the Holy Spirit does the works of God in you. He will complete it. Philippians 1:6 says, "He who has begun a good work in you will complete it until the day of Jesus Christ." (NKJV) Hold on to this promise.

BEGIN TODAY—IN THE HERE AND NOW

Now is the time and place God has designed for you to begin. Directed by the Holy Spirit, begin to give to others what God gives to you whenever you can. Give in confidence and faith, knowing that investing in people is an eternal investment. Remember the words of Jesus in Matthew 6:19-21.

> *Do not store up for yourselves treasures on earth, where moth and rust destroy, and where thieves break in and steal. But store up for yourselves treasures in heaven, where moth and rust do not destroy, and where thieves do not break in and steal. For where your treasure is, there your heart will be also.*

I encourage you to make encouraging others a way of life. Encouragement is the soil in which closer mentoring relationships will grow. Love to rub shoulders with people who want to learn how to hear from God; always seek to encourage them: we do. Wherever we are, we seek connections with others and look for ways to encourage them. It doesn't matter if we are on the road or at home, if we are giving to our own children or to other people's children, to our personal friends and close neighbors or to those in our small group. Encouraging others to listen for Jesus' lovely voice is an honor. Serving people at the International House of Prayer is a pleasure. We love being on the team.

BE FLEXIBLE AND PATIENT

We have mentored more in some seasons than in others. Some years we've traveled and received opportunities to impact people away from our home area. Other years our sphere of influence has been closer to home, centered within our family, neighborhood, and church. We try to remain obedient to where the Lord is leading us. In my "tent making" business, I sometimes need a helping hand. That has brought many opportunities to encourage young people, helping them to earn a few dollars or just having an excuse to be with them, to listen, share, build friendship, and love on them. Whatever small part we play, it is satisfying to us.

Recently my free time has been devoted to writing this booklet and working on another book, so I haven't been as accessible to others as I normally like to be.

Don't be discouraged if you can't find a mentor right away. As you continue seeking the right person for yourself, keep asking God to teach you. He wants to help you mature. Nurture your hunger for more of God and His divine connections. While you wait, be a mentor to someone else! Begin to read books by prophetic people; each writer will impact you differently. Granted, books cannot substitute for the face-to-face opportunity to talk and ask questions. But each book will discuss a different facet of prophecy, and you'll learn from all.

If you attend prophetic conferences, I have a suggestion.

If there is ministry time, go to the front and listen to the words being spoken over people. Listen as intercessors pray with God's heart and resonate with the Holy Spirit; learn to pray with the Spirit in your own prayer life. It is interesting to hear how different people pray truth and prophesy. Watch for the release of the Holy Spirit. You will begin to learn how uniquely He works in others and how He wants to work in and through you. These are significant lessons.

If you can't attend a conference, look for someone in your local church to mentor you. Ask your pastor or an elder you trust and respect.

TRUST THE RESULTS TO GOD

You many never know the impact you make on someone that you mentor. Have you ever heard of Edward Kimball? There is a good chance you might be a direct result of his mentoring. Edward was a Sunday school teacher in the eighteen hundreds. He was committed to reaching the lost youth in his classes. He was particularly burdened for one young man. When describing the youth, Kimball said,

> *I have seen few persons whose minds are spiritually darker when he came in my class, or one who seemed more unlikely to become a Christian, still less likely to fill any sphere of public usefulness.* (A.P. Fitt, *The Life of D. L. Moody* [Chicago: Moody Press, 1976], 23)

This young man went on to become known as a spiritual pioneer in modern techniques of mass evangelism. This man impacted Rev. F. B. Meyer, who later touched J. Wilber Chapman, who led Billy Sunday to Christ, who then converted Mordecai Ham, who in turn led many teenagers to Christ in North Carolina, including Billy Graham. Only heaven will reveal the actual number of people reached through the result of Edward Kimball's humble efforts when he led Dwight Moody to the Lord!

A SPIRITUAL INVESTMENT

Mentors are great at seeing the potential within you and making an investment in your life. I'd like to share a story with you that is a great example of how a pastor became a cheerleader for a younger man. Don Finto served as the senior pastor of Belmont Church in Nashville, Tennessee for twenty-five years and is now the head of Caleb Company. This story is about his relationship with the musician and singer Michael W. Smith. For twenty years, before Michael W. Smith cut any records, Pastor Finto laughed, cried, worshiped, prayed and traveled with Michael in a father-son type relationship. "I could write a book about Finto," Smith says. "He's my daddy in the Lord. I don't think I'd be where I am today if it hadn't been for Don." Finto now serves as a pastor to pastors. "I am an encourager," Finto admits. "I can often see more in people than they can see in themselves, and I want to call it forth in the name of the Lord." The effect of his ministry gift on Smith has been profound. "I've saved all my letters from him, all the little note cards," Smith says. "He has encouraged me in so many ways—my self-confidence and who I am in the Lord—pulling stuff out of me that nobody ever was able to pull out."

Do you have a desire to mentor others? Just do it! Reach out today to build a friendship with someone who needs encouragement in the Lord. I can't think of any higher calling than empowering people to help them build the Kingdom. I challenge you to pass along the skills, talents, and abilities that

God has given you. I applaud you and your efforts to roll up your sleeves and help teach younger people about prophetic ministry. The impact you can make in one person's life is staggering. Where should you start? Just get involved in the life of someone around you. The rest is easy!

RECOMMENDED READING

Mike Bickle, *Growing in the Prophetic* (Lake Mary, FL: Charisma House, 1996)

Bobb Biehl, *Mentoring* (Nashville: Broadman and Holman, 1996)

A.P. Fitt, *The Life of D. L. Moody* (Chicago: Moody Press, 1976)

Jim Goll, *The Beginner's Guide to Hearing God* (Scottsdale, AZ: Regal, 2004)

Paul Stanley and Robert Clinton, *Connecting* (Colorado Springs, CO: NavPress, 1992)

Jimmy Stewart, author of the article "The Man Behind Michael," *Charisma*, April 2000, pg. 54-55

ABOUT THE AUTHOR

On New Year's Eve in 1993, the Holy Spirit surprised John O'Shaughnessy by giving him the gift of prophecy. That beautiful Spirit of Truth who filled Jesus began to change John's life and the life of his family forever. You can read about John and Caryl's story in their upcoming autobiography, scheduled to come out early in 2009.

Following God and led by the Holy Spirit, John and his family exchanged a comfortable life in a Midwestern suburb for a life of uncertainty. They relocated to Kansas City in 1994 and found a new church home in Metro Christian Fellowship. They received their ordination in 1998 from Grace Ministries. Their obedience did not lead to traditional Christian service. John's friends and parents, even John himself, might have understood if he had become a missionary or a pastor. It was harder to understand when the Holy Spirit led him to deliver telephone directories, paint houses, and start an itinerant prophetic ministry. Through many difficulties, John practiced listening for the voice of God. He determined to follow Jesus, wherever He might lead—into a marketplace ministry as a house painter, through the discomforts of platform ministry, in the joy of serving family groups in his church, and into the difficulty of writing a book out of obedience to God. John says, "I'm not a writer but I began to write out of obedience."

God watches over men and women who are looking for Him, not for easy ways. He gives them treasures of the spirit that can't be bought with the coin of this realm. As John and Caryl have freely received, they continue to freely give. Currently they are serving as small group leaders and prophetic mentors at the International House of Prayer in Kansas City, Missouri.

AUTHOR'S NOTE

It's my hope and prayer that after reading this booklet you will want to be more like Jesus. Hearing God's voice is for everyone, not just a few people. Perhaps your heart is stirred to have someone mentor you (or your small group) in the prophetic, or you want to mentor someone else. Either way, I believe it's God's desire that you take the next step. We would be honored if you told a friend about our booklet so that the truths contained here would be passed on to help another person. If you have a group of people who want to be mentored in the prophetic, please contact us. Arrangements can be made for John to come on a regular, semi-regular, or occasional basis to help encourage you to grow in the prophetic. Contact us and we will give you the requirements relating to ministry trips.

If you would like to contact John and Caryl for additional information, please do so by writing them at:

Praiseworthy Ministry
P.O. Box 461
Grandview, MO 64030

To sign up for updates, please e-mail us at:
praiseworthyministry@kc.rr.com

www.praiseworthyministry.com

To order additional copies of this booklet, complete the order form on the last page.

BE ENCOURAGED

Order Form

Booklet	Qty	Price	Total
Be Encouraged	_____	$4.50	_____

Subtotal: _____

Shipping. Add 20% (minimum $3.00): _____
Tax. (Missouri residents add 7.85%): _____
Total enclosed (U.S. funds only): _____

Your Name: _____

Address: _____

City, State, Zip: _____

E-mail address: _____

Send payment with order to:
Praiseworthy Ministry
P.O. Box 461
Grandview, MO 64030